Songs of Going South

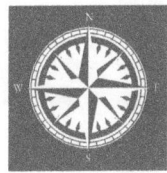

Siddharth Mehrotra

SULIS
P R E S S

An Imprint of Sulis International Press
Los Angeles | Dallas | London

SONGS OF GOING SOUTH
Copyright ©2025 by Siddharth Mehrotra. All rights reserved.

All rights reserved. No part of this book may be reproduced in any form or by any means without the prior written consent of the Publisher, excepting brief quotes used in reviews.

ISBN (print): 978-1-958139-57-8
ISBN (eBook): 978-1-958139-58-5

Published by Sulis Press
An Imprint of Sulis International
Los Angeles | Dallas | London

www.sulisinternational.com

Contents

Summer's Day 1
Lonely Cloud 3
To a day after a night of rain 4
Autumn Sunset 5
Mountain Path 6
The Search 8
Boxing Match 9
Divine Wind 1 11
Divine Wind 2 12
Divine Wind 3 14
Divine Wind 4 16
Divine Wind 5 17
Divine Wind 6 19
Stave-clash 20
Wisdom of the Ages 22
Fairytale Voyage 23
Lines of Battle 24
Haunted Wood 25
Bristlecone Pine 27
Ghost Forest 28
Summer Storm 29
Desert in bloom 30
Rocky Mountain Height 32
Vale of Paradoxes 33
Rain-lashed canyon 34
Dakota Plains 35
Storm over Prairie 36
Winter Gale 38
Brahmashira (the divine weapon) 39
The Heavenly Cockerel 41
The Big-game Hunter 42

The Unicorn 44
The Unicorn fights the Viper 46
Verse against Evil....................................47
Marshes at evening 48
The Snapping-turtle.................................50
Dust Storms...51
Summer Hillside 53
Rural Florida 54
Shipping on the Mississippi.....................55
Caribbean Sunrise 57
Island-hopping...58
Wizards' duel 60
Archmages Opposed...............................61
Vampyrum spectrum 63
The Eagle Owl..64
Dragon's boast 65
Indricotherium/Baluchitherium 67
Healing the land.......................................68
The Magic Wand......................................70
Flood lines 71
Soaring Peak 72
The house-mouse....................................73
Ferret 74
Axe and Sabre 75
Nicole's Boast..76
The Sack of Castle Crag..........................78
The New Deluge 80

Summer's Day

The breeze was soft,
the brakes were calm;
The land's green robe
lay lush and long.
Eddies spun
in the otter's-road;
Warm winds whistled
among willow-withes.
Every tree rang
with the trill of songbirds;
Speckled salmon
sported in the streams.
Old eagles soared
in the upper air;
Lizards lazed
in the light-drenched stones.
Bees and butterflies
browsed among blossoms;
Hart and hind
in hedgerows hid.
Crab-spiders lurked
in coreopsis,
Spread their claws,
to spring on the bees;
Ladybirds trundled
up ladderlike stems,
To batten on the aphids
who bled the plant.
Hawk-moths hovered
in the heat of the day;
Swifts and swallows
swept over rivers.
Piebald calves

played in the pastures;
Coyote's cubs
in the copse cavorted.
Banks and brakes
basked in the sunshine;
Mountain and meadow
were mantled in light.

Lonely Cloud

Adrift in the winds'-way,
dragon-shaped,
Softly spreading,
snowy-shining,
incongruous
in the clear sky,
Breeze-borne alone,
from its brethren sundered,
Lonely on high
over lofty peaks.

To a day after a night of rain

> Water works wonders
> in this world of ours,
> From shimmering clouds
> in the sheer morning air
> To gleaming pools
> on glossy roads.

Autumn Sunset

Fading day
unfurls its banners,
Blue and gold
on the bright Heaven;
Then rolls them up
in ruby-colored ribbons
And sets them aside
on star-spangled sable.
The pearl of the night
glows palest green
Through the veil unrolled
by the westering day.

Mountain Path

Soaring summits
on the sinister side;
Darksome depths
on the dexter hand.
Soaring summits
to the sun's-path ascended;
Darksome depths
plunged to Death's domain.
Sharp breezes sashayed
among sheer drops;
Bright the fair-wheel
in the blazing sky.
Eagles cried
in the upper air;
Larks sang alarms
in lower lands.
Rock-rabbits romped
on ragged aretes;
Lizards lay
on lighted ledges.
Every summit seemed
to stay the sun;
Every chasm seemed a path
to the core of the world.
Passes lay poised
between peak and pit;
Roads awry,
like roots, around rocks.
The sun's-path was full
of snow-capp'd mountains;
Crisp cold streams
ran crystal-clear.
Light breezes caressed

the blossoming fields;
Meadows gleamed
with multitudes of flowers.
Slabs of stone
shone slaty-blue;
Pine-trees seemed
to pierce the peaks'-pane.

The Search

"They gazed from every mountain
    height,
Searched each cavern black as night,
And wandered through the flower'd
    shade
By pool and river and cascade";
Down city streets and country roads,
O'er deserts hot and glaciers cold;
From fairy isles in furthest west,
To Appalachian mountains' crest,
From Yukon's evergreen-mantled hills,
To Rio Grande and its lesser rills;
But, though they sought in every place,
Of Nicole, they found no trace.
Their errand they told
    to all they met;
Their purpose they named
    to people everywhere.
"Over many an ancient river, and many a
    palmy plain",
They searched and sought and
    overturned through sun and wind and
    rain.

Boxing Match

Masters of the art
are a marvellous sight;
The wise in warfare
are wondrous to behold.
Like strong bulls striking
with their steely horns,
And brazen flanks
broadsides exchanging;
As antelopes,
or antlered moor-treaders,
Who deal out dints
for the dark-eyed doe;
Like warring greylags,
their wing-shoulders bristling,
Matching their might
for maidens' sake;
Like bold male kangaroos,
balanced on their tails,
Their hind-feet flying,
hitting hard,
With pounding kicks
competing for power:
Fire leaps
from flailing fists,
Cloud-light blazes
from clashing shins.
The brazen sky shuddered
at the blows they aimed;
The dints by them dealt
stirred dust and sand.
The wind-blown alighted
on the warriors' limbs;
The fine-grained settled

on the fighters' shoulders,
Where it brightened both
their beauteous heads
And shot shimmering rays
from the shoulders of the heroes.

Divine Wind 1

The black wind; the red wind;
the blight-wind; the ill-wind;
The wind that whirls
at the walks of the dead;
The foggy wind
and the fiery wind;
The earthquake-wind
and the answerer's call.
Trees were toppled
and towers crumbled;
Shingles and wall-beams
were showered afar.
It was the worst storm
they had ever withstood;
The blasts of driven sand
were blinding!

Divine Wind 2

The black wind; the red wind;
the blight-wind; the ill-wind;
The woeful storm
and the withering gale;
The turning wrath
and the terrible blast;
The wind that whirls
at the walks of the dead;
The foggy wind
and the fiery wind;
The earthquake-wind
and the answerer's call.
It rang on walls
and rattled windows;
It dried deep lakes
and drenched dry land.
Trees tilted;
towers trembled;
Fires in flues
refused to flame.
The land shuddered;
lakes touched the light's-path;
Rain-kites fled,
ragged and rent.
Lightning flashed,
lights blew out;
Shingles fell,
shutters clattered.
It was the worst storm
we ever withstood!
The blasts of driven sand
were blinding!
When the furor had cleared,

our friends were lost;
When the bluster ceased,
they were blown off course.

Divine Wind 3

The black wind; the red wind;
the blight-wind; the ill-wind;
The woeful storm
and the withering gale;
The turning wrath
and the terrible blast;
The wind that whirls
at the walks of the dead;
The foggy wind
and the fiery wind;
The earthquake-wind
and the answerer's call.
Trees toppled,
towers tilted;
Streams ran backward,
stars seemed to tremble.
Red dust arose
to darken the sun's-road;
Lightning flashed
in a lightless welkin.
Hailstones fell
from the height above;
Quavers shook
the wide-breast below.
City and country
suffered alike;
Buildings whistled
and branches roared.
It was the worst storm
we ever withstood!
The blasts of driven sand
were blinding!
Aircraft were grounded

and their ends diverted;
Traffic stopped,
and lamps turned on at noon.
When the furor had cleared,
our friends were lost;
When the bluster ceased,
they were blown off course.

Divine Wind 4

The black wind; the red wind;
the blight-wind; the ill-wind;
The woeful storm
and the withering gale;
The turning wrath
and the terrible blast;
The wind that whirls
at the walks of the dead;
The foggy wind
and the fiery wind;
The earthquake-wind
and the answerer's call.
Walls were broken
and woods overturned;
The foam-course stopped,
and fled up-stream.
It was the worst storm
we ever withstood!
The blasts of driven sand
were blinding!
When the furor had cleared,
our friends were lost;
When the bluster ceased,
they were blown off course.

Divine Wind 5

The black wind; the red wind;
the blight-wind; the ill-wind;
The woeful storm
and the withering gale;
The turning wrath
and the terrible blast;
The wind that whirls
at the walks of the dead;
The foggy wind
and the fiery wind;
The earthquake-wind
and the answerer's call.
It tore up trees
and toppled towers,
It shattered windows
and shook down tiles;
It splintered posts
and spilt boiling cauldrons,
It wailed through houses
like a woeful phantom,
It froze the ground
and flattened the five grains.
A veil of dust
overwashed the winds'-way;
Grey grew the land;
all the ground became ashen.
Curtains flapped
like a conqueror's banners;
Fires faded
to fitful flickers.
It was the worst storm
we ever withstood!
The blasts of driven sand

were blinding!
When the furor had cleared,
our friends were lost;
When the bluster ceased,
they were blown off course.

Divine Wind 6

The black wind; the red wind;
the blight-wind; the ill-wind;
The woeful storm
and the withering gale;
The turning wrath
and the terrible blast;
The wind that whirls
at the walks of the dead;
The foggy wind
and the fiery wind;
The earthquake-wind
and the answerer's call.
It tore up trees
and toppled towers,
It shattered windows
and shook down tiles;
It splintered posts
and spilt boiling cauldrons,
It wailed through houses
like a woeful phantom.
It hardened hearts
and made husbands cruel,
It froze the ground
and set friends at feud.
A veil of dust
overwashed the winds'-way;
Greenish it glowed
in the gathering gloam.
It was the worst storm
we had ever withstood;
The blasts of driven sand
were blinding!

Stave-clash

The deadly pole-axe!
The wizard's staff!
The deadly pole-axe
danced like a fire;
The wizard's staff whirled like a
    windmill.
Back and forth
bounded the battlers bold;
Side to side
sprang the swift sword-stormers.
The square-sky plunged
like a squire of thunder;
The staff arose
like a striking sea-serpent.
The cutlass-clashers
belched clouds and mist;
Their groans and cries
alarmed ghosts and gods.
Their battle-cries
made the broad Earth tremble;
Their stamps and shouts
made the stones to dance.
The nine-tailed lash!
The wizard's wand!
The lash of nine tails
like a lightning-bolt;
The wizard's wand
like a whale breaching.
The lash raught out
to lacerate limbs;
The staff stretched forth
to strike upon heads.
Red drops ran

down the rawhide whip;
Sparks arose
from the spike of the rod.
Back and forth
went battle-birds' gladdeners;
Right and left
they reaped a grim harvest.

Wisdom of the Ages

All things that are, someday shall not be;
All that is not, someday shall be;
All that shall be, someday shall not be;
And all that shall not, shall be again.
"There is no safety, and there is no end".
Hope and Despair are both futile;
Be steadfast in truth, and the good shall approach you.

Fairytale Voyage

        Upon Sunset Sea
        Past the Gates of Eve
        Amid the Cloud-Islands
        At the Edge of things
        On the Tides of Time
        And on waves of gold.

Lines of Battle

The weapon-storm fell
like whitecaps breaking;
The light arose
like levin in reverse.
Like all-burning flame
at the end of the world,
Like Destroyer's trident
as Time concludes,
Those deadly weapons
dazzled and danced;
Those fearful instruments
flashed and flared.
All the world seemed to tremble,
both waters and mountains;
All the upward shuddered,
and the eye of day darkened.
Helms were cloven,
hands were severed,
Armour pierced,
edges dulled,
Blasters broken,
bones laid bare,
Shields were split,
shafts lay shattered,
Rockets were crushed,
ray-guns pulverized,
Explosives were bled,
poisons emptied,
Gasses were spent,
greaves were split,
Staves were splinter'd,
standards tumbled.

Haunted Wood

Necromancers:
'Now is the hour:
as night approaches;
As withdraws the sun,
let dreams haste hither!
Let every tree watch
with eyes a-blaze;
Let the crevasses gape
as cavernous maws;
Let the breeze, leaf-laden
through the branches quivering
Turn crooked boughs
into clutching talons,
Hollow oaks
into howling phantoms,
Weeping willows
into wicked witches,
Glow-worms into
a ghoulish gaze,
And the shadows of palms
into sharp-toothed monsters;
Let a fall from the bank
into foaming shallows
Turn rotten logs
into ravenous caimans
Slippery soil
into pseudo-ophidians
And tatter'd roots
into terrible tentacles;
Let fear and terror
follow him everywhere,
Let horrors harry
and haunt him endlessly!'.

Within the hour, he leapt to his feet and
   ran about like a young elephant in
   breeding-season, and trampled all in
   his path.
Every tree watched him
with eyes a-blaze;
Crevasses gaped
as cavernous maws;
The breeze, leaf-laden
through the branches quivering
Turned crooked boughs
into clutching talons,
Hollow oaks
into howling phantoms,
Weeping willows
into wicked witches,
Glow-worms into
a ghoulish gaze,
And the shadows of palms
into sharp-toothed monsters;
A fall from the bank
into foaming shallows
Turned rotten logs
into ravenous caimans,
Slippery soil
into pseudo-ophidians,
And tatter'd roots
into terrible tentacles;
Fear and terror
followed him everywhere,
While horrors harried
and haunted him endlessly.

Bristlecone Pine

Lonely stood
the little tree,
Alone atop
a lofty eminence,
Since ancient days
when the Earth was young:
It sprouted
when the space divided,
When the plain parted ways
with the path of the moon,
When heaviness sank
and the heavens ascended.
The last of its kind,
it lingered on high;
First and last
of a forest long vanished.

Ghost Forest

As pollution thickened, the air grew warmer;
As the air grew warmer, the glaciers melted;
As the glaciers melted, the oceans rose;
As the oceans rose, the woodlands were flooded;
As the woodlands were flooded, the trees perished.
As pollution weakens, the air grows cooler;
As the air grows cooler, the glaciers renew;
As the glaciers renew, the oceans sink;
As the oceans sink, the marshes are drained;
As the marshes are drained, the trees may grow again.
Neither good nor evil can conquer for ever.

Summer Storm

> Clouds burst
> in a clash of thunder;
> Rain rattled down
> on the reddish stone.
> Canyons filled
> with crag-carving currents;
> Vale and waterway
> whitened with foam.
> The cloud-drops fell
> in a clattering clamour;
> Heavenly waters
> hammered down hard.
> Crags came loose
> and crashed into the currents;
> Rocks went rolling
> down river-beds.
> Brimming brooks
> ran brightest crimson;
> Swirling streams
> filled with scarlet sand.
> Flat land filled
> with feathery froth;
> Basins brimmed
> with bursting bubbles.
> The wasteland was wrapped
> in a watery veil;
> The red land donned
> a robe of silver.
> Land and its limits
> were lost in confusion;
> The world was one mighty wavering
> mass!

Desert in bloom

As the heroes of the dawn
drove the host of darkness
into the deepest nooks
and darkest crannies,
Fiery flags
flew far and wide,
Purple-gold pennants
appeared on all sides.
Soaring silks
of scarlet and crimson,
Weather-might whirled
in waves over winds'-way.
The desert bloomed;
the dry land blossomed;
The barrens yielded
to bright flowers springing.
Sleeping seeds
swelled and arose;
From dormant dust
rose a dazzling dance.
The mother of the Titans
was mantled anew,
In a rainbow of hues,
from the red dunes leaping.
The golden-brown
shone green and blue,
Scarlet sands
glistened silver and jade;
Pallid shrubs
shimmered purple and golden:
Multiple colours
in motley array,
Together gleaming

in glorious profusion.
Sweetness and spices
scented the air,
From yucca-flowers
and younger plants sprouting;
Cacti played
upon curling trumpets,
Thorn-bushes bloomed
in thronging spires.
Birds, bats, and butterflies
burrowed into blossoms
And pulled their heads free
pollen-covered.

Rocky Mountain Height

The path was narrow;
the peaks touched the moon's-way;
The high road hung
in the hollows of the hills.
The brazen breeze-highway
shone bright and cloudless,
An eye-aching upward,
of indigo's colour.
Shrill-criers soared
over sheer escarpments;
Bough-headed moor-treaders
bugled in the vales.
Startling outcrops
stood out sharply;
Bluish masses
raised their brows from the slope.
Our heroes crested
hill after hill,
Our friends fared onward
over fir-clad fells,
Capp'd with snow
and cloaked in trees,
With blossoms bright
under a blazing sun.

Vale of Paradoxes

Dead trees upright
upon dazzling green,
The Evergreen name
dishonour'd forever;
Snow in summer
silver on the summits,
Glaciers' tracks
grey and gaping;
Gleaming daylight
glittered on the green-gold,
Beside brightest clouds
casting blackest shadows.

Rain-lashed canyon

Pattering, puddling, pounding
from the peaks'-pane;
Rattling, ramping, rapping
on the road-beds;
Clattering, clamouring,
clapping on the cliffs;
Whorling, whirling,
washing down valleys.
Crags were carved
and canyons were deepened;
Rocks washed away
in the rills turned to rivers.
The churning was charged
with the chalk of the hillsides;
The burn was blackened
with blossoming earth;
White was the wash
with the willow-withes;
The tarns were tanned
by the trees torn down.
Flowers rode
on the foaming flow:
A wedding-procession
for the wives of Faunus.
The floodgates of Heaven
seemed flung wide open;
The roads themselves ran
like rivers in spate.

Dakota Plains

Silver webs covered
the sea of grass,
Warp and weft
over verdant waves,
Unto two-and-thirty points
in ten directions,
Mile after mile
across mountless plain.
Elk strode the pampas
with antlers aloft;
Bison plodded
like boulders rolling.
Bulrush sloughs
full of blackbirds and butterflies,
Waves of grain
as wide as the horizons;
Golden miles
and gleaming greenery,
Rolling hectares
like ripples in the earth.
Not a hill, not a tree,
between Heaven and Earth;
Flat land lay
under fiery sky.
From dawn to dusk
was dazzling brightness;
From set to rise
was a sea of stars.
Atmosphere shone
over endless fields;
Golden grain waved
under gleaming airs.

Storm over Prairie

As our friends lingered on the fruited
    plain,
the air became hot and still,
and the sunshine too bright to look upon.
Helms of hiding gathered under the
    dripping hall,
and the troposphere became full of
    masses of dun-coloured
    cumulonimbus,
in the shapes of anvils, towers, castles,
air-borne cities and spired cathedrals
pointed arches and fearsome gargoyles.
After two double-hours of stillness,
a ripple ran over rows of grain,
and thunder followed.
All the shelters of birds
were shaken in the gale;
The raven's path trembled
in the roaring gusts.
Every flower and frument
fell flat before the furor;
Birds and beasts bowed
before the blustering blast.
Darkness fell;
day turned to night;
Sky-flames flashed
like skeletons dancing.
Thunder and trumpets
thrummed through the heartland;
The shaper of rain-kites
shook the horizons.
Then came the rain:
Sheets and shafts

of shining showers;
Javelins enough
of rejuvenator of soil.
It fell in columns
like flag-staves of chariots;
It plunged from the pinnacle
in pillars and pyramids.
The clamour of this sort lasted a day and
    a night, whereafter the prairie and its
    cities shone like jewels newly
    polished.
Each colour and shape
stood clearer and deeper;
Every line on the land
more lucid than before.
Buds came open
on battered blossoms;
Steam arose
from stone and soil.
Birdsong swelled
from boughs and brakes;
Bullocks and bison
belled with relief.

Winter Gale

It froze the field
and felled tall trees,
It bred black ice
and bruised blue boulders,
It ensnared trout in streams,
bade them sleep for a season,
It dropped birds from the air
and broke bottles on door-steps.
Day's disc became pale,
and the dark arrived early;
The ground was as iron,
and the grass grey and sere.
Leaves fell en masse
from lofty boughs,
Blackened at once,
to be borne on bare earth.
Songbirds fell silent,
turned to stone in their sorrows,
Boulders cracked
and boughs exploded.
Wolves cried out
on a wasted day,
Honey-pawed hooded-ones
hid in their hollows.
The beam roved about
with a booming roar,
One way and another
over wide-bosomed Earth;
It infiltered in furrows
of frozen soil,
Overturned in an instant,
and tipped with rime.

Brahmashira (the divine weapon)

Seeing this missile
assembled and aimed,
With the dreadful white-mouth
drawn and ready,
All living things
of every kind,
All animals and plants
between Earth and Heaven
Grew terrified
and turned their backs,
And fled with loud cries
into the foliage to hide.
Trees with their boughs
trembled and tossed,
The winds ran wild
and whirled about.
It touched the world's helm
with terrible flames
And blazed in a sphere
of blinding splendour.
All furred and feathered
were filled with dread;
All green and growing
groaned in terror.
All the Heavens blazed
for our heroes' sake,
All the roads were alight
for the rescuers' discomfort:
Clouds rang out
countless clamours;
Stones fell from Heaven,
and the star-road trembled.
The three worlds were lit

by a thousand suns;
All the welkin filled
with woeful noise.
The breeze-way was hidden
by a blinding blaze,
and linden-light shone
over land and wave.
The winds'-way trembled,
the wide-path shook;
Streams churned,
stones shuddered.
The weeds of the hills
were warped out of shape;
Branches quivered,
boles were broken.
Thunder crashed,
winds thrown together;
The broad ground blazed
with a blinding radiance.
The canopy shook,
and canted awry;
Willowy boughs
tossed wildly in the whirl.
Birds and beasts
fled blindly away;
Earth and air
filled with echoes of their cries.
All creatures cowered
from that crackling light,
The fiery javelin,
fearsome to all.

The Heavenly Cockerel

His head in height
was Heaven's equal;
His feet were founded
in the furthest abyss.
His coral-hued combs
were as curtain-walls;
His dark eyes
as the depths of space.
His bill was a blade
of sharp burnished bronze;
His wattles and dewlaps,
the war-gear of heroes.
His long slender limbs
were as lapis lazuli;
His toes were tipped
with talons of diamond.
When he raised his wings,
all realms took notice;
When he cried aloud,
all creatures heard.

The Big-game Hunter

His red cheeks were swollen
like ripe tomatoes;
His lips were strangers
to lightness and laughter.
He had keen blue eyes
and a crooked nose,
Smoke on his breath,
and a small bristly moustache.
His stout frame was clad
in stainless white,
And a pith-helm was perched
on his depilated pate.
His hairy arms
bore heavy hands,
Grasping and hard,
with grimy nails;
The soles of his feet
wore seven-league boots,
Scoured by the sand
of seasons of slaughter.
He toted a rifle
with two blue barrels,
With a steely lock
and a stock of ebony.
A fine cord encircled
his fat greasy neck,
And a single brass bullet
was strung upon it.
Furred, finned, and feathered
alike fled from him;
A fiend was he
to all four-footed creatures.
At the stamp of his feet,

they startled and hid;
When he raised his gun,
they ran and perished.

The Unicorn

Light-stepping runner
on lofty mountains;
Fleet-footed in flight
over fruited plains.
Night-eyed, silver-hooved,
nimble sky-dancer;
Cloudy-maned moon-child
of colours five.
His flanks are a mule's
of finest breed;
His purple head
is a pillar's top.
Rage shines forth
from his ruby eyes;
Gently he goes
on jewelled feet.
From his brow breaks his horn,
like a beacon's beam:
Sable and crimson,
silver and golden.
The point thereof
renders poison harmless;
Its light kindles kindness
in loveless hearts.
One stroke of his hooves,
makes streams to flow;
The touch of his horn
cleanses tarns of contamination.
He rends the wind's kites,
to bring rain in the drought;
He fights off fiends,
to defend the helpess.
All fair things affect him,

and all foul things fear him.
Mighty is he
in all matters of arms;
For he suffers none
to seize him alive.

The Unicorn fights the Viper

With horn and hooves
he hammered his enemy;
With brow and boot-land
he beat him down.
The long legs smote
like lightning-bolts;
The hard hooves fell
like heaven's spears.
The serpent rose
like a sea in spate;
The forestmaster plunged
like a fire of Heaven.
The coiling one belched out
coloured fogs;
The seeker exhaled
a silver mist.
The hisses of one
made the Heavens shake;
The neighs of the other
made the netherworlds tremble.

Verse against Evil

In the name of the Nine,
By the martyred snails
By the Sudarshan Disc
By Indra's Arrow
By the Mark of Good
By the Runes of Odin
By the Fire of Behram, the first and brightest,
By the Light of Heaven, that illuminates all:
Do we cast out evil
Do we banish the Falsehood
Do we conquer the ego
Do we vanquish the selfish
Do we overcome pride
Do we smother hatred
Do we extinguish anger
And bring peace to the anxious!

Marshes at evening

Broad and bleak,
by brooks divided;
Rank and dense
with reeds and saw-grasses.
Mantles of moss
masked the meres;
Curtains of earth-sighing
cloaked the currents.
Werelights winked
in the watery winds;
Lanterns fit
for the little people.
Woodpeckers tapped
at waterlogged bark;
Lovelorn frogs
sang loud and lustily.
Midges hummed,
menace to mortals;
Mosquitoes sang,
conquerors of kings.
Bitterns boomed
in the banks of reeds;
Herons stood vigil
on the highest branches.
Weather-tellers
watched for minnows;
Duckweed-lions
danced in the depth.
Ravens rang out
their rattling calls;
Thickets thrummed
with throstle-song.
Dragonflies darted

over dazzling pools;
Beetles bustled
in the bubbling springs.
Mayflies leapt
into momentary life;
Caddisflies uncoiled
from crystal cocoons.
As the orb's endless spin hid the eye of
    day
And the candles of night were enkindled
    on the clouds'-street,
Green light shone in the greyish ground-
    grief
And bobbed about in the boles and
    boughs.
Water burned with werelights after
    hours;
Birds cried warnings from broken
    branches.

The Snapping-turtle

A mossy carapace,
one meter across;
A heavy head,
and hard-edged jaws.
Blazing eyes
in a black brow burning;
Claw-tipped flippers
clove the calm of the current.
A red tongue flashed
between ridged jaws;
A tiny flame
in a tenebrous cavern.
Where he lay on the lake-bed,
he eluded all eyes;
Where he bit, he held
until black clouds gathered.
A wonder of the world
revealed itself:
The snapping-turtle
of the swampland pond.

Dust Storms

Mountains of menace
mantled the moon's-way,
And dust-clouds rose
to darken the horizon.
"They overtook cars
and out-ran trains;
Airplanes fell
from the endless sky".
Fires danced
on farmers' fences,
And batteries burst
into balls of lightning.
Kine and coursers
were killed where they stood,
Shocked out of life
by the shining of the storm.
Turnips and potatoes
were torn to pieces,
The five grains, and maize,
caught aflame where they stood,
Pease and pulse
were pulverized in an instant,
Beans and bulbs
were burnt to ashes.
Sand devoured
the soft rich loam;
Black soil churned
into barren redness.
None could distinguish
night and day;
The weather-world
wore a Western mourning.
The sullied rivers

grew sluggish and slimed;
Dust fell like snow
on the decks of ships.

Summer Hillside

Its steep sides rose
to the stormy star-path;
Its rounded flanks
seemed to reach the horizon.
Menacing clouds
hid the mountain-top;
Rain ran in rivulets
to the roots of the rise.
Eagles called
on the airy heights;
Robins sang
in the rushy glen.
Snow capped the peaks,
despite summer's heat;
Broad-boughed trees
blossomed below.

Rural Florida

Water-cars floated,
weightless-seeming,
Still and steady
on stone-lined streams;
Keel-deer passed
over canopy unhindered,
And floated free
among fleecy clouds.
Mist arose
from mangrove-woodlands,
And crocodiles lurked
in crooked streams.

Shipping on the Mississippi

Ships all around,
all shapes and sizes,
Boats and vessels,
big and small,
Hover-crafts
and hydrofoils,
Helicopters
and humming sunplanes,
Air-borne kites
and outboard motors,
Paddle-boats
and pinnaces,
Keelboats, carracks,
and cargo-tugs,
Punts for lone pilots,
and ponderous carriers.
A thicket of thole-deer
thronged the way-swift;
Countless craft
crowded the currents,
From the least of punts
to the largest of liners,
From sleek small sailboats
to slow solemn sunships,
Packed and piled,
prow to port-hole,
Stem to stern,
steerboard to broadside,
As one craft moving,
the wide waves seeking,
Line upon line,
for the lord of the rivers,
Down the pike-road

to the Dawnlit Tide,
On the swift steed's back
toward Sunrise Sea.

Caribbean Sunrise

A golden ship
came gliding over,
Too bright its captain
for the bare pupil:
With staves of ring-flame
stretched over stanchions,
With poles of cave-fire
in pinnaces'-path.
He churned the deep
into challenge-colour,
Beat the brine
into burnished hue:
With a rosy blush
o'er the rim of the world;
From pole to pole
shone pearly-pink;
Then spread and shifted
to a sparkling brightness,
And deserved the name
of Sunrise Waters.

Island-hopping

Like doomed souls
from death to death,
Like the unenlightened,
ever reborn,
Like little birds
from limb to limb,
Like locusts hopping
leaf to leaf,
Over the ocean,
from island to island,
Our heroes flew
from hill to hill,
Each a shining green star
in the shimmering blue,
A little bright jewel
in the low-lying currents:
Cuba hight,
cradle of farmland;
Wooded Jamaica,
the wellspring isle;
Haiti-Kiskeya,
home of peaks;
Boriken, Rich Port,
brave lord's isle;
Anguilla, isle
of the Arrow-shaped Serpent;
St. Martin's Oualichi,
mount of salt;
St. Christopher's Island,
crop-bearing country;
Our Lady of Snow,
land of fair waters;
Montserrat,

realm of many-thorned bushes;
Light-named Barbuda,
land of herons;
Antigua, island
of the taking of fish-oil;
Guadeloupe,
of the limpid streams;
Dominica
the lofty land;
Martinique,
of many flowers;
St. Lucia,
the lizards' dwelling;
St. Vincent's Isle,
vale of the bless'd;
Barbados,
of bared reef-teeth;
Trinidad hight,
the hummingbirds' home;
Tobago last,
of burning incense.

Wizards' duel

The Hammer of the Mind
felled the Hand of Death;
The Blinding Dark yielded
to Blazing Light.
The Arrow of Acid
fell on Aerial Armour;
The Wave of Earth
met the Reversal Charm.
The Pillar of Flame
plunged into water;
The Force-Lash failed to offend,
and faded.
The Shower-of-Arrows
pierced the Shield of Saturn;
The Halberd of Light
scored the Hand of Despair.
The combatants looked
like two clouds pouring rain;
Their wizardries shone
like the weapon of Jove.

Archmages Opposed

The fiend-routing blade
faced the fiery claws:
The 'Laughter of the Moon'
against the 'Lord of Darkness',
The 'Dragon's Talons'
against the 'Dreadful Thought'.
The glaive rose skyward
like a growing tree;
The talons descended
like toppling towers.
The blade shone forth
like a blazing meteorite;
The claws unfolded
like corn-cutting sickles.
One stroke of the steel
can start quakes and tremors;
Once the nails take hold,
they never release it.
The dragon-man cried:
'Withdraw with honour!';
The liar answered:
'Look to your life!'.
The flame-serpent called:
'You must free our friends!';
The nithling answered:
'It is none of your business!'.
The striker flashed
like streaks of lightning;
The bill fought back
like a bolt of flame.
Between fire and lightning,
who can find a victor?

Between blaze and thunderbolt,
who bears the prize?

Vampyrum spectrum

Night incarnate,
whom none could conquer;
Darkness embodied,
death's own herald.
Fine fingers spread
into furry wings;
Curved claws tipped
the coal-coloured vanes.
Razor-edged teeth
like ceramic knives
Too large by far
for the lipless mouth.
Brow-stars blazing
like bright-burning gledes;
Ears attuned
to echolocation.
A wonder indeed
of the wider world:
The single species
of spectral-bat.

The Eagle Owl

Midnight hunter,
Minerva's companion,
Flower-faced flier,
feathery-footed,
Of blazing eyes
and a bill like a blade;
And soft-tasselled wings,
soundless in flight.
No shadow too deep
for his shining gaze;
No sound escapes
his slitted ears.
His head when it turns
describes half-a-circle;
If he leans far enough,
he can look straight backward.
Dusk to dawn,
he dallies with the air,
His eyes alight
and ears ever open.
A menace he
to mice and rats;
The eagle-owl
of ancient lineage.

Dragon's boast

I am stronger than lightning;
stones crack before me;
Waters part,
and the winds are scattered!
My scales shine
in the stars every night,
My voice is heard
in the wildest blows,
My trifurcate tongue,
electricity's self!
When I clap my wings,
the clouds gather;
Let me breathe a little,
and I bring the rain.
I was born from a stone
on the banks of a river;
When I rose to heaven,
the rains poured down.
Where my shadow falls,
there is shade for hours;
Where my claws pierce the ground,
there is clean black soil.
I can plough hectares
and pull down peaks;
I can smother a wildfire
and smell ten years' scent.
Harpoons and javelins
break their points against me;
Set a hook in my jaw,
and I can haul you off!
Shield and armor
shatter before me;
I can blow away

both blade and blaster.
What powers of yours
compare with me?
What strength have you
to set against mine?
I can raise the round Earth
and rend it asunder;
If I hit too hard,
the Heavens open.
'Tis your time of truth,
if you try for my treasure;
If you frighten my friends,
your fate is sealed!

Indricotherium/Baluchitherium

        A towering herbivore,
        taller than trees;
        A leaf-eating giant,
        more lofty than mountains.
        Four legs span
        the furthest horizons;
        A long neck reaches
        the lightsome canopy.
        Ears upright
        turn in every direction;
        A fingered lip
        defoils the forest.
        Truly a wonder
        of times long ago:
        The aullay-beast
        of the Oligocene.

Healing the land

He sang fine new trees,
fresh and beautiful,
Of dewy blossoms
and dark rich soil,
Golden with grain,
garnished with fruit-trees,
Full of bright flowers,
flourishing colour,
Of gentle breeze
and young birds carolling,
Of holy meres
hidden under stone,
Of starlit nights
after sunny days,
The chirrup of birds,
and the chants of votaries,
The ripples of rivulets,
the rush of rapids,
"The whistles and thrums
of the whirling winds",
The swelling echoes
of silver bells,
The crackling of ice
at the coming of spring,
The rumble and roil
of rocks underground,
The high-pitch'd hum
of the honey-bees hovering,
The secret silence
of softest snow,
Of smokeless blazes
in sacred places,
Flaming on,

no fuel demanding,
Of stylites feeling
in a state of grace,
Penitents certain
their pasts surpassed,
New songs come
of novice composers,
Scientists thrilled
by sudden discoveries,
Logicians and geometers
overjoyed by their theorems,
Fauns and elves dancing
with fairy maidens,
Children at play
with good cheer in their voices,
Pollution cleansed
and lands at peace.

The Magic Wand

The rod in my hand is of rare woods
    indeed;
The wand I hold is of wondrous power!
It was fashioned from a tree
of the fruit immortal;
It was taken from the boughs of the Tree
    of Life.
The Lady Queen Mother was lord of the
    garden,
The Goddess of Youth was guard at its
    gates,
When this trunk was planted
in the triple heavens,
When this sapling sprouted from the soil
    of the true source,
In ancient times in the orchard of the
    gods,
In the Mountains of Jade where
    immortals dwelt.
In its youth it stood
by the Jasper Pool,
Its growth was tended by godly maidens.
I cut it with a golden sickle,
carved nights and days with a knife of
    jade,
and filled it at last with force enough
for taming tigers and subduing dragons,
spinning straw into gold and turning
    stones into mushrooms.

Flood lines

Floods came down
a flagpole thick;
Purple columns
pillar-broad.
Masses of weather-might
mounted up,
Piled in the peaks-pane
like pinnacles of mountains.
Flashes flared
in the folds of the wind-kites;
Dazzlers shone
in the dark hiding-helms.
Silver streams
soaked the slopes;
Rivers arose,
overran their ramparts.
The dry earth shuddered,
drenched to the bone;
Roots and rocks
were eroded to ribbons.

Soaring Peak

Soaring peak
and sloping sides,
Base as broad
as both horizons;
Snow-capped summit
silver-gleaming,
Cloud-capped foot-hills,
crystal-glistening.
Its pinnacle arose
to pierce the peaks'-pane;
Its sides swelled
from sunrise to sunset.
Shrill-criers soared
among sheer crests;
Monkeys chattered
on its mantle of leaves.
The bright-disc's road
harboured birds and bats;
Vines and roots
concealed vipers and pythons.
Furnished the fells
with flowers many,
And healing herbs
on the heights all-a-glow.
Fairies danced
on the fairest foot-hills;
Sages sat
before simple huts.
Cooling breeze
on the crags cavorted;
Silver mist
sailed softly overhead.

The house-mouse

Crumb-snatcher's kinsman,
Quern-licker's offspring,
Burrow-dweller,
Bread-nibbler's grandchild,
Of scaly tail
and scurrying paws,
Quivering nose
and quavering whiskers,
Ears like clovers
and eyes like black gems,
Nut-gnawing teeth
and night-dark coat.
No fear hath she
of fire-taming men,
But nips at their heels
and nibbles their grain.

Ferret

On crooked claws,
the cunning mouse-catcher;
On racer's legs,
the rabbit-hunter:
Narrow-faced,
of nightly habits,
Black-footed, buff-coated,
burrow-raider;
A menace indeed
to mice and marmots;
Terror to rats
even twice his size.

Axe and Sabre

The soft-horned falls,
to sever Earth's bones;
The cutlass rises,
to crack the fair-roof.
The power-span falls,
to oppress the neck's burden;
The blood-grip rises,
to blunt evil's edge.
The hewer waved,
shaking Heaven and Earth;
The quencher stirred
both the quick and the dead.
One was the minion,
wicked and foolish;
The other the teacher,
eager and wise.
The foul fiend tries
to defend the god's house;
The lie-hater seeks
to liberate friends.
The battle-bright fell
like a bolt from above;
The draw-wand rose
like a dragon from the sea.
The rage of their sword-storm
split rocks and felled trees;
The clamour of their club-clash
filled clouds with thunder.

Nicole's Boast

Nicole raised her chin,
curled her lip,
She tossed her brown locks
and told as follows:
'Our ways of life
were too widely apart,
Our manners too different
to permit of our friendship.
You would draw me back
to dreams and shadows,
You would tie me again
to pretence and fancy,
To "other worlds",
as empty as ashes,
To fantasy-lands
as fragile as soap-bubbles;
But my eyes are set
on the actual world,
And my limbs depend
on reliable things.
There is more in that
than your magic can give you;
Truth lies only
in the tried and tested.
I have walked on the worlds
we wished to visit,
And stood in the light
of the stars they orbit:
Those points of light
we played at visiting,
Those tiny sparks
we pretended to name,
I have seen as Suns

in skies of their own;
I have walked on the worlds
awash in their light.
Fact has given
that Fantasy promised,
And Reality given
all its Opposite offered;
By work and toil
I have won my awards,
By regular effort
I have raught all mine ends,
That you tried to have
by tricks and by-ways,
That ever you sought
by the easy way.
But I know you too well:
you are never content;
I understand you,
who always want more:
'Til you draw out my heart,
you will not dream of rest;
'Til you drink my blood,
you will drag this talk onward'.

The Sack of Castle Crag

Ten thousand years Crag Castle stood;
  In an evil hour, its ages were ended.
Ten thousand armies on the threshhold
    perished;
  One final blast laid the fundaments
    bare.
Ten thousand weapons broke on the
    walls;
  A single shot overturned them in
    ashes.
Soaring towers and solid walls,
Mighty battlements, mead-halls massive,
High stone walls stood hundreds of
    years,
In solitary splendour on the summit's-
    shoulder.
None knows who built it; their names
    are lost;
Who lived below, no lore recalls.
What wars they waged, the wise alone
    know;
What peace they enjoyed, only prophets
    can tell.
Long it stood among lofty peaks,
With watchful eye on the valleys below.
Never the fort had known defeat,
Save only once; it was empty ever after.
Bats and doves on the barbican nested;
Ravens roosted on the ruined keep.
Now again came on a grim defeat,
An end of glory in after times.
Our heroes took holt in the hollowed
    halls,
Our friends refuged in the fortified zone,
With their hated enemies in hot pursuit,

With the crooked-schemers close behind.
The warlocks ringed the walls about,
All the forces of evil, with flames in hand;
Then lowered their wands to light the fire,
In blackest dust from the bowels of the Earth.
The cannon spoke in cruel accents,
Words of woe, to bring walls to wreck.
Forward leapt the fiery shot,
Red-hot iron, ruin bringing.
In heart-rending shock as if Heaven had fallen,
In an almighty crash like the end of the world,
Portal and portcullis in pieces fell;
Towers and walls came all tumbling down.
Pulverized rock painted the peaks'-pane;
Smog and ashes smothered silver streams.
Mourning cries made the mountains shake;
Woebegone wailing rang valleys like bells.

The New Deluge

Old mariners marvelled
at the main above them;
Seasoned sailors stared
at the skies beneath them.
The hyaline rose
to heights unrecorded;
the main descended
in a mighty crash.
The green ground groaned
as if the globe were ruptured;
the oceans roared
from their innermost depths.
The flowing winds shrieked
with the fury of a cyclone;
A dazzling radiance
dimmed the stars.
One instant, the ocean
seemed emptied of its waters,
Then flooded in the next
with a foaming surge.
Foam and froth
filled the vales;
The mere overbore
the mountaintops.
It washed the valleys
from West to East;
It soaked the summits
from South to North:
Spilling, rushing,
splashing, gushing,
Until creeks were o'erborne
and continents buried.
The flow filled the valleys
and "flooded the rain-clouds".

Clearer than crystal,
it closed every crevasse;
As mighty as Fate,
it mounted to Heaven.
The mere had o'ertaken
the Mane of the Field;
The land was concealed
by the Lord of the Rivers.
The Waverer filled
with a watery scent;
Fresh was the whistler
with fumes of the froth.
One looked in vain
for the land all around;
One sought without hope
for a sight of the shore.

About the Author

If you benefited from this book, please consider posting an online review. Thank you in advance.

Siddharth is a prolific writer of poetry and fiction, and holds a Master's degree in critical comparative scriptures. He lives in California immersed in his study of ancient texts and mythologies, the search for planets in outer space, and a lifelong practice of Tae Kwon Do.

Visit the author's website at
https://www.imagesinwords.net/images-in-words

About the Publisher

Sulis International Press publishes select fiction and nonfiction in a variety of genres under four imprints:

- Riversong Books (fiction)
- Sulis Press (general nonfiction)
- Keledei Publications (spirituality)
- Sulis Academic Press (academic works)
-

For more, visit the website at
https://sulisinternational.com

Subscribe to the newsletter at
https://sulisinternational.com/subscribe/

Follow on social media
https://www.facebook.com/SulisInternational
https://twitter.com/Sulis_Intl
https://www.pinterest.com/Sulis_Intl/
https://www.instagram.com/sulis_international/

www.ingramcontent.com/pod-product-compliance
Lightning Source LLC
LaVergne TN
LVHW091316080426
835510LV00007B/512